SPIRITLINE

REFLECTIONS FROM THE SOUL

Liberty Communications Press

SpiritLine

Reflections from the Soul

by Nancy Rathbun Scott

ISBN 0-9664391-0-4
LIBRARY OF CONGRESS
CATALOG NUMBER 98-96183

Published in the United States of America

ACKNOWLEDGEMENTS

WITH HEARTFELT GRATITUDE AND LOVE,
SPIRITLINE IS DEDICATED TO THOSE WHO HAVE
SHARED THE TEN GREAT LESSONS ...

MIKE, WHO GUIDED ME TO THE VALUE OF
TRUTH ...

JENNY, WHO TAUGHT ME ABOUT
UNCONDITIONAL LOVE ...

MY FATHER, WHO PROMPTED
UNCOMPROMISING **SELF-VALUE ...**

MY MOTHER, WHO UNDERSTOOD THE VALUE
OF **DISCIPLINE ...**

BETSY. WHO, EVERY DAY AND MORE THAN SHE
KNOWS, SHOWS **PATIENCE ...**

HENRY. WHO HAS FOUND THE SERENITY OF
OBEDIENCE ...

LAURIE, WHO SETTLED FOR NOTHING LESS
THAN **FREEDOM ...**

MICHAEL, FOR TEACHING THE PEACE OF
FORGIVENESS ...

LOUIS, FOR UNFORGETTABLE WORDS OF
TRUST ...

DERYCK. FOR LESSONS IN **JOY ...**

AND FOR THEIR ONGOING
GUIDANCE, LOVE AND SUPPORT—
KAREN, MARTHA, PHYLLIS,
PRISCILLA AND CINDY

SpiritLine's cover, designed by Nancy Rathbun Scott, features "The Day," a painting by Italian metaphysical painter Gaetano Previati (1852-1920).
The blue symbol is Nancy's adaptation of "Aum," Hinduism's sacred symbol of the Source of All.

ASPIRATION

In my life
There can be Truth.

In my work,
I can honor God.

I can speak softly
And politely. . .
Be gentle and genuine.

ॐ

My Gift

I am not perfect and I am not wealthy,
But I can give to everyone I meet three things:

Encouragement
Affirmation
Energy

WHO AM I?

I am a soul evolving. I am an angel. I am perfect and becoming more perfect. I am energy and love and light.

I am thankful and grateful. I am searching, probing, seeking, prepared.

Sometimes I fear, but I persevere.

I am what I do, but I am so much more. I am what I can do, what I dream to do, what I envision.

I am complete now, but open and ready to be filled, to experience and to take in.

Every moment invigorates me: good moments and bad moments.

I am not God, but I am of God.

THE BOOK OF SECRETS YOU'VE ALWAYS KNOWN

All will be revealed, though not perfectly.

You will see Truth as she is,
Not as you would like her to be.

Live by the Golden Rule.
Extend love to every living thing.
Comfort and connect.

Not lonely.
Not alone.

This is God's promise.

Say "I-Ying."

The mantra, I-Ying,
Means nothing
And everything.

God will hear your need.
Trust that.

ASSIGNMENT

Fill yourself with Light
And go shine.

RELATIVE SIZE

My ego minds being judged
But Davida, My Soul,
Is too large even to comprehend.

ॐ

CREATING

What we think,
Is the beginning of
What we do.

What we do
Is who we are
Beginning to be.

FINDING GOD

The more I know about love,
The more I know about God.

If I want to know about God,
I learn all I can about love.

Practice it.
Find ways to express it.
Look for it in unexpected places.
Honor it in every area of life.

God waits.

To Honor

Davida, My Soul, chooses to stay with Little Me
Until it is time to go.

"Little One, I love you.
I protect you always.
Never Fear."

No wonder I ask,
"What can I do in this lifetime,
With this body,
On behalf of My Soul Davida?"

My Soul's Covenant

Be of peaceful spirit.
Accept and love and give comfort.
You are free.

The day is new.
You have come to this place by choice
And the outcome is ordained and incredible.

Keep listening.
Be still.

I am with you.
Beside you.
Inside you.
Of you.

My Little One.

BALANCED

Calm follows effort.
Effort follows calm.

Lost in thought.
Found in stillness.

GIVE UP!

My mind says, "Don't give up!"
My soul whispers "Give...
Give UP!"

STILL

The answer lies in stillness.
Only in stillness.

Listen to your inner voice.
It is always there.
Quiet.
Faithful.
Waiting.

Full of wisdom
From ages and ages and ages
Beyond knowing.

GOD'S ORCHESTRA

It's so simple.
Meditation is listening—
Listening to God.

Just before the orchestra begins,
I am ripe with anticipation.
Not thinking or knowing what to expect.

Simply listening.
With all my heart and mind and body.

Can I listen to God
Any less fervently?

INSIDE

Take my sight down into darkness.
Everything that has ever lived,
Lives still.

THE WAY

I love...
I am loved.

I heal...
I am healed.

This is the Law:

We are what we do
And so much more.

VERY TRYING

Effort is ridiculous.
Everything of value and of essence
Happens in stillness.

LISTEN TO THE FEELING

Our bodies
Are the instruments
Of Remembrance.

SHY

My inner voice says:
If you ask me to speak
Be prepared to listen.

But before you listen
You must hear.

Open your own throat,
Not to speak to others.
But to speak to yourself.

When you don't speak aloud,
Perhaps
You are not yet prepared to hear.

ADVENTURE

On the edge of nausea
On the verge of discovery.

AT LAST

I no longer need pain
To experience joy.

I can heal myself any time,
Every time.

My choices are boundless
My possibilities endless.
My probabilities limitless
My realities multiple.
My future manifest.
My love farthest reaching.
My energy universal.
My hope Truth.
My Truth eternal.

I am god.
I am of God
I am One With God.

I no longer need to hurt
To experience love.

REMEMBER

You are not broken.
You are learning.

ॐ

LIGHT

From my god to your god.
From the god within me
To the god within you.

Dripping away fear and doubt.

MORNING

I am blessed
By the Rosy Crimson
Of Gratitude.

And breathe
With the Body Cosmos.

THIS MORNING

I stand in gratitude for
This lifetime.
This opportunity
To serve and
To learn.

EGO

Let go of your wonderfulness.

TEMPLE

Let not your body
Be a burden in this lifetime of service.

But, rather,
Make your body light,
Strong,
Soft,
Healing,
True.

DIS-EASE

Listen with respect
To your dis-ease.
It has been growing for a long time
And speaks very softly.

When you say to your dis-ease,
"Ah, now I know,"
Sometimes it goes peacefully
Into that good night...
Heard.
Acknowledged.
Honored.

At last.

I think
All it ever wanted
Was a little audience.

AUM

I hear eternal music
In the pitter-patter
Of every raindrop
That ever fell.

POTENTIAL

If it seems necessary,
It also is possible.

MASK

When we mask fear
We do not see fear
For what it is.
And, therefore,
Learn naught.

FOR TODAY...

Suspend Disbelief.

BLESSING

See inside other people
And forgive.

See inside other people
All the way to their grace.

Colors

Fear lifted its gray quilt
And left me with the
Silver mist of possibility.

TELLING TALES

I am The One who watches
The one who is doing.

Apparently, I have decided to stress myself.
Why would I do such a thing?

Stress pushes me,
Rocks me,
Sickens me.
Stress passes for progress.

If I listen, stress is a road map
And not entirely useless.

STEP ASIDE

The sights, the sounds, the breath of life—
All are contained in this body.

The purpose and the intent
Are contained in this Soul.

When we fight our innate will, we suffer dis-ease.
Surrender, yield, trust, have faith.
And the Glorious Will can manifest.

Learn to trust your own Will. It is infallible.

But how can I know my Will?

You need not "know" it at all, for it is not of the
mind. Simply allow it to be.
(This is less about marching
And more about stepping aside.)

Get out of Will's way!

THE HOME STATE

Grace...
A state of bliss.
A state of loving transmission.
A good state to be in,
Not from.

DEVOTION

Devotion does
No matter what.

Devotion learns
In doing.

Doing in devotion
Brings results
That never happen
When we do for fun.

MOTHER GOD

I will take care of everything.
Believe.

I always have, haven't I?

You will have a wonderful place to live
And delicious food to eat
And love,
Lots of love in your life.

I will take care of everything.
Believe.

NOTHING?

God be with me.
God be in me.
I know God through my own acts.

I heal myself so that I can trust myself
To heal others.

I know God not by "nothing,"
But by being still.

I need not go to "nowhere,"
I need only to listen.

No-Body
Doing No-Thing?

No.
This body,
Feeling and listening.

I know God through my own acts.
I learn God in each lifetime,
Not for amusement,
But for Love.

Love enriches the All.
God wants me happy.

MONEY

The universe has given you
Money.
And will give you more.

You must repay the Universe
In other ways.

PRAYER

My hands are healing hands.
My words are healing words.
My love is healing love.
My faith is healing faith.
My heart's a healing heart,
My voice a healing voice,
My place a healing place

My part,
The Whole.
The Ever-Ever Universe.

In God.
In Truth.
In All.

Amen.

OFF THE HOOK

If I rush to repair you
And am successful,
You will only need to break down
When I'm not available.

Fixing is changing
And that can only happen
At the core.

When I remove your challenge,
I take away your tools
For learning.

STILLNESS

I come to meditation
Expecting to heal, to see, to know.
And nothing happens.

Turn over these meditations to God!
She knows what I need.

Do not expect.
Do not judge.
Do not hope.
Rather, wait.
And wait again.
Be still and watch.

Still is all I need to be.

INDUSTRIAL STRENGTH, INDUSTRIAL THOUGHT

Industrial Strength is the power to do, to make, to materialize.

But the meaningless chant I-Ying intones for that which cannot be articulated, let alone "done." I-Ying is a matter of surrender, of faith in the good directions of God.

It's not what is said, but what is *thought* about what is said that matters. Such is the nature of reverse speech, words tape-recorded and played backwards. Senseless, but—it has been said—full of wisdom. Such is the nature of all words, which are the ensuing stage of thought.

Purify thought and only good can endure.

SERENITY

Be true in your heart.

Ask not of other ways,
But respect unto your own.

Take heart.

Do not envy.
Do not blame.
Do not anticipate what you cannot know.

Take, instead, the road that suits you best
And walk up it well.

STRUGGLING IN THE ARMS OF GOD

I cry, "Only for a moment with God!"
Ha!

She is everywhere
And, so,
Too large for me to perceive
With senses or intellect.

Still, I can rest within Her.
(What's the use, though, if I'm struggling?)

I NEED, I GET

I am already realized.
I receive from the meditations what I need.
The thoughts are messages from God.

Intent makes all the difference.

When I come to God intent on hearing, I hear.
When I come to God intent on healing, I heal.
When I come to God intent on peace, peace abides.

She knows.
Why do I keep forgetting?

Einstein Says To Me...

Inward bound
Is outward bound.

FRIENDSHIP

My Friend,
My intent must be always to honor you.
To honor your will and your intent.
But, most of all,
To honor God within you.

It Takes All Kinds

We try to take God
And stuff her into
Our small lives.

She won't fit.

We grow to hate the cacophony of our minds.
But ecstasy and despair share the search for God.
They are bonded travelers in the journey.

DISCOVERY

Negative energy—
I produce it, not observe it.

The sound of that voice,
That presence
And my whole body freezes with negative energy.

Prompted from without?
No, I make it.

So couldn't I make another energy?

Yes I could.
I can.

(I just haven't remembered how.)

I know how,
But I've forgotten.

Discovery.
It's reacquainting ourselves with what we know.

SKY DIVING

I must do the things I am afraid of
So that I can do
All the things I want to do.

VIBRATION

If I don't vibrate with pain, I don't hurt.
If I don't vibrate with dis-ease, I heal.

When I vibrate with health, I am whole.
When I vibrate with goodness, I am serene.

To change it,
To be it,
Vibrate with it.
Simple.

I know pain's vibration.
I know misery's vibration.
I know fear's vibration.
I know mistrust's vibration.

Do not vibrate there.
Then you will vibrate elsewhere.
And you will learn.
And you will know.

ॐ

Surrender the Day

"Seize the day!" The phrase has an imperative about it.

A softer thought occurred. Surrender the Day.

No imperative. Just the determination to surrender narrow, personal ambitions and, instead, "will to will" for the highest good of all concerned (which also includes me!).

SNOWFLAKES

Would anyone be interested in the meandering of
my mind?

Perhaps.
Because it is the Cosmic Mind.
The Universal Mind.

What's different is I sometimes write.
To observe. To notice.

My filter is just a little discrete,
A little distinct.
Your filter pattern is your own, too.
Your own snowflake filter
So everything comes out a wee bit different.

Snowflakes
Look primarily alike.
But then you've got
Wet snowflakes and
Powder snowflakes and ice,
Dripping
Huge
Dashes
Across the Sky.

Put on your snowflakes
And meander through the universe.

GRATITUDE

Word for today:

Gratitude.

Gratitude for today.
Gratitude for the moment.

In the candle;
In the honeysuckle;
In the vine and the vacuum
And all between.

Gratitude.

And I can spread it.
Not by saying,
But by noticing.
By paying attention.

Look everywhere.
And know.

TAKE IT EASY

Rest.
Rest assured.
Rest easy,
Rest along,
Rest comfortably,
Rest stop.
Stop.

Stop worrying.
Stop projecting the earthiness.
Outward is inward.

The earthiness is only that.
Inside is the You-ness.

Therein lies all of it.

Since you create your own reality
You cannot be unhappy.
You do not want this for yourself.

Been there.
Done that.
Not now.

Instead
Devotion.
Commitment.

You Were Beautiful When You Smiled

My mother thought she had bad teeth. She was born in 1910 before dentists could fix absolutely anything and I suppose a few of her top teeth did bend slightly to the left or right. It was hard to tell, because she simply wouldn't smile a toothy smile.

In 1988, she had a stroke and, following some time in a nursing home, she died at our house. In those last days before death, Mother forgot she had bad teeth. A sort of luminance took over her skin and eyes and she smiled absolutely all the time. Fully smiled, all those crooked teeth showing. It was dazzling.

On her birthday this year—nine years after her passing—I wrote a little something for Mom that said:

My Dearest Mother:

There you are, next to me. You smile proudly. You hold my hand. You were not always perfect, but when you became yourself, you were beautiful.

MISERY'S LESSON

Of misery, I have heard this:
You cannot know joy without suffering.

The more suffering you understand,
The more you understand suffering.
And the more joy you see, too.

This is not a system of rewards,
Not an earned pay-off.
There is no karmic debt.
There is no payment.

Only there is awareness.

Welcome all of it.
And watch.

COMPLAINTS

My head is killing me (with static).
I can't bend over (or submit).
My neck is stiff (in one viewpoint).
I'm exhausted (and tired of everything).
My eyes are running (like tears).
I'm coughing up (my life).

How much more articulate
Does my body
Have to be?

THE PROMISE

My Soul speaks to me of fowl
And the fish that float in the mire—

Those Above and those Below;
The Spirits here and the Spirits there.

I have much to do, says my Soul;
Much to accomplish,
Things to set straight.
And I can.

These things will be shown to me,
For I have the wisdom to see.

BLESS YOUR ENEMY

You ask much of Your Fowl.
She can sing of many things,
But mostly of This:

Do not be afraid,
For your fear
Is only the woodpecker,
One who makes a huge racket,
But is of no consequence.

You fly on wings
And snatch the mouse and the bat.
You take even the civet
To feed your young.

Nature does abide.
And you, too,
Little One,
Abide in your nature,
Which is:

Strong and watchful and gentle and quiet.
But which does what needs doing,
And parries with the one who needs parrying.

Fly high
Among the pines.
Sit feathered
along the branch.

Smell the wet trees
And feel the sun sparks
Along the forest floor.

You are of The Owl.
White and huge and lovely.

Your enemy is weak in this lifetime.
But he is learning much.
Learning to be strong, to be fair,
To be balanced.
To take the simple with the complex.
(It is all the same.)

He teaches you courage
And persistence
And belief in The Way as The Way.

Without him, you could not have known.

Bless this well and fly high.

NOTHING TO FORGIVE

I was angry with you—one that I love—and I was having a hard time "forgiving" (much less forgetting). I'd been mistreated, disregarded, forgotten, I thought.

But I'd played a part in the problem, too, having behaved rather badly myself. The guilt made it worse and I was stuck in suffering.

Both of us needed forgiveness, it seemed. But then I looked differently.

Perhaps there was nothing to "forgive,"
Because there was no sin.

No betrayal, because
Your love was as perfect as you could give
And I accepted it—and you—
In free choice.

The anger and guilt faded
And I knew.

Before we "forgive" others,
We learn to "forgive" ourselves.

ॐ

73

BE WHAT YOU WANT

Even if I did not have
The Perfect Mother,
I can be The Perfect Mother.

I can bring her inside of me
And pour her out.

And then I have The Perfect Mother
After all.

ॐ

HOLOGRAMS OF GOD

The technology of holograms is pretty amazing. Each holographic piece embodies all the elements of the whole from which it came. Each holographic remnant contains the original picture.

In one sense, the remnant is the complete picture. In another sense, it's a mere fraction...but it's a perfect fraction, a whole fraction, a fraction exactly like every other fraction—no better, no worse, no different—but, at the same time, very different, because each fraction is separate from another. Puzzling, isn't it?

You can destroy any single piece of the hologram and the original will remain intact. In fact, you can destroy all the prints and copies and pieces, and the original will still remain intact. But, without the original, the very image that was, will, one day, be no more.

Can you scar one piece? Of course. But it won't change the others. You can even turn and twist individual pieces, making each appear different. But, in essence, each stubbornly remains the same as every other...a true embodiment of the original.

Do you want to see what the master original looks like? You can look at the holographic remnant and get a pretty good idea (miniature, constricted, narrow, but reflective, sort of). Given how the world batters stuff, though, you'll have to overlook the dents and scratches, the turns and twists. You'll have to focus—really focus with determination (and faith)—on the original image.

If you like what you see there, you'll surely like the Master, too. But if you don't like what you see in that one piece, you won't like what you see in any other piece either.

Amazing how our view of ourselves affects our view of others.

VEGGIE LIGHT

A friend became a vegetarian because he wanted to be lighter in every way possible.

Light-headed.
Light-hearted.

In-Light-In-d.

INITIATION

Rapid change is coming and it cannot be stopped. Be prepared. It will feel like a fall.

But you will fly.

The key is to let go of stubborn old ways. These caused misery and depression. But you have won and it is time to greet the sun.

Your tools are faith and trust. Wonderful things are starting to happen. You are blessed with cosmic energy to change what needs to be changed. The step has been taken.

You sit at the center of it all, calmly. People are drawn to you. And all that you wish for will be yours: joy in all things.

How? Because the seeds of success and triumph are taking root.

You will receive what you have earned.

ॐ

DREAMS INTO THE AIR

Did any little—let alone big—thing ever materialize in this world without having been spoken first? Can we make events come to pass without first putting words to the thoughts?

The best things in life sprout from the loveliest thoughts shared aloud. (The darkest deeds, too, follow the spoken word. Enough said.)

We needn't speak our good to another person— not necessarily. But perhaps we must speak it, at least, to ourselves (not merely think it; speak it). And if we want our joy to grow and grow, it helps to say so often. Why is this?

Words have energy—physical energy. They agitate the air and make waves. They create movement and flow. They reverberate. They reach others. (Thoughts do these things too, but, for most of us, telepathy is harder, slower.)

Words have power. They strike a special covenant within our hearts, among other people, and with God. Who knows why. Who cares?

Words precede physical action. They may not command physical action, but—without words—few (no?) thoughts go forward into execution.

Have a great idea? Say it to yourself, out loud. Say it out loud often. Then, say it to someone else. Better yet, say it to several someone elses.

Say your idea, out loud, to many someone elses often, and watch it happen.

I KNOW A FEW THINGS

I know God is good.
I know music is divine.
I know animals think.
I know I love.
I know love is stronger than evil.
I know healing makes me smile.
I know change is growth.
I know peace is stillness.
I know giving is receiving.
I know light is pure.
I know service is holy.
I know I am more than I see or think.
I know what I think is not who I am.
I know I live beyond death.
I know the earth is divine.
I know I have lived before.
I know grace shows.
I know I have a purpose.
I know I have forgotten more than I'll learn.
I know I have a choice.

BONDING OVER PEARS BRULÉ

I think I may have met Linda's baby last night. At least, I had a profound sense of him about the time dessert arrived.

I didn't think of this baby in personal terms at first—not when Linda told me she was seven weeks pregnant. "Mostly it's scary," she said.

I suggested that a baby probably changes your life "for the better."

Linda looked at her lap. "But I like my life." (Linda and her husband do have a large measure of the "good life".)

That's about the time I had a sense that this baby might have reached down and plucked Linda and her busy life right out of the universe...seeing right past all those blackened Day Timer pages, right through to Linda's heart...seeing that Linda would rather be doing something else with her days, but she can't (won't)...not just yet, anyway.

She might need a compelling reason.

Just before the pears brulé, I may have met him.

MANTRA ALL

God speaks to me each day through the mantra,
I-Ying.

I wasn't hearing.
It was too simple.

I-ying.
I listen.
I balance.
I see.
I surrender.
I yearn.
I absorb.

These are all God's voice.
And millions more.

THE SOUND OF FOREVER

I wonder what Forever sounds like.

Maybe like creation. Noiseless, but emphatic.

Maybe—like creation—Forever happens in the splinter of time it takes to dream something up or get an idea. Bingo! Whoosh! Yowie! Forever appears...with shape and form and a whole lot of instructions...but no fracas.

How about before that instant of creation, though—before that frozen fracture in "time," when creation tiptoes into existence? Isn't Forever like that, too? Not merely possible, but inevitable— even when we don't hear it coming?

Forever: waiting, in the stillness, through all the moments and eons, even when we're deaf to it.

Like creation,
It's never not been there.

Forever soundless.

GOD DOESN'T NEED ME

When Jenny was born, I fell in love. That worked out pretty well because my baby needed care that drew upon my mental, emotional, physical, and spiritual resources.

It didn't matter whether Jenny loved me or not. To be the mother I wanted to be, I needed to love her. For that task, my devotion to Jenny was essential.

Maybe God doesn't need me to love Her, either. But, in order to be my own personal best, I need to love The One Higher than myself.

Why else would I take time to be quiet, or reflect, or renew myself? Why else would I practice the only devotion that pours back to, nourishes, and advances me?

God may not need me to honor Her.
But if I don't, how will I grow?

Churning

Are you broken?
I can't tell.

But better stop
And not fix that which appears splintered.
Perhaps your solutions are in the churning.

THE PAIN-FULL METAPHOR

No need to prove this.
No need even to believe this to make it work.
I'll just listen to my next physical complaint
And notice that, perhaps, pain is an illusion
To help me describe my current circumstances.

INTENT ON MEDITATING

I come to meditation intent on listening to God.
Thoughts intrude and I am frustrated.

Why?
Isn't that what I wanted?

These are not idle thoughts.
They are God's voice.
Intent makes it so.

Live intentionally.

ॐ

GREEN

I heal myself every day
With the beauty that surrounds me.

WITH AFORETHOUGHT

"Aforethought." In the law, it seems, we're not guilty unless we decide, in advance, to be bad. Otherwise, the crime is something of a cosmic accident. Don't all our actions fall under the same rules of serendipity?

In order to make destiny or desire materialize, first we must do something. I think our souls are waiting to deliver on the promise, but first we must act. And before that, think.

We must act with intent.

Do I want to be a novelist? Then first I must write a novel (if I write a poem, I will not be a novelist).

Do I want to be famous? Then first I must open myself to the many (if I shroud myself in privacy, I won't become famous).

Do I want to be considered beautiful? (Or do I want to be beautiful; there's a difference, I think). Then first I must behave like I imagine beautiful people behave (if I choose the wrong model, the results won't satisfy me).

Our souls wait to deliver.
Let us act, therefore, with aforethought.

ASK THE RIGHT QUESTION

Why am I here?
What should I be doing?

Wrong question.

Instead, ask:
"What do I learn from my discontent?"

TELL ME

Are there any questions to which Love is not the answer?

ॐ

HANDING OFF TO GOD

My friend, Trish, had an Epiphany. "I just threw myself down on the bed and said, 'That's it, God. I can't deal with this anymore. You take it.'"

When the Epiphany occurred, Trish's life was a mess. Her soon-to-be-ex-husband was rattling swords. She didn't have enough money to pay the rent. She hated where she lived. She had a rash of pains and physical ailments. Her job was going nowhere. She was scared.

When she finally handed the mess to God, the act was not one of withdrawal. It was more like surrender. Trish decided to stop struggling against the tide and float to shore (drowning never occurred to her).

But there was plenty of uncertainty. She didn't know how far out to sea she was. She didn't even know which ocean she was in. She didn't know where she'd come ashore or whether she'd like the place she landed. She only knew that for right now—for today—she was going to accept where she was, spread out her arms and legs, and go with the tides.

ॐ

Trish didn't expect to feel "happy." She just accepted that her highest good was being tended to. Also, she decided to consider whatever possibilities whispered her way. Her state of mind changed almost immediately. "I felt relaxed—even joyful. All of the sudden, I was excited. I couldn't wait to find out what was on the way."

What happened?

In the end, Trish says, "I want what I got."

LUST AND TRUST

To give oneself over in lust, we need not trust the other. But we surely must trust ourselves. In doing so, we stay safe and no harm can come.

What does it mean to trust oneself? Only this:

Will we love ourselves after?
Will we continue to walk on our own true path?
Will we hold fast to our own vital self-interest?
Will we augment our own life's purpose?
Will we fall, weak and limp, or arise stronger?
Will we abandon ourselves to mere reflection,
Or will we vibrate with new energy?

When we answer according to our hearts, then we do not break trust with ourselves and, thus, we are free to love another.

LOVE

You are his woman.
Your fire is his fire.
Your light, his light.
Your flow, his flow.
Your shadow, his shadow;
Your flicker, his flicker.

You are a mirror in all things.

What he sees in himself, he sees in you.
Though what he sees in you,
He does not yet see in himself.

IRRESPONSIBLE

What I do
Isn't changing you.
What I do
is changing me.

My father didn't love me
And he never would.
Realization of "truth?"
No.
Change in perception when I finally said,
"It didn't have anything to do with me."

More change when I finally said,
In a way, it had everything to do with me.
(The thinking he didn't love me? Mine.
The thinking he never would? Mine.)

That's when the change took place.
In learning only to observe.
Only to take notice.
Only to say, "Oh. So that's how it is. Okay."

The liberation comes, finally,
When we are no longer hell- nor heaven-bent
On outcomes from the other.

OCEANS OF AIR

I sit beside the ocean
And hear God breathe.

THE KING OF NOW

The Past, Present and Future—
All live in my mind.
Where do I want to be?

Always in the moment
For it's the one of three
I rule.

KICKING TO BEAT THE BAND

Life is not a struggle.
Life is.

What we do inside life may
Feel like a struggle...

Our hearts beat fast
We pace and moan.
Our minds race and groan—
Flail, kick, shudder!

What happens when we stop?

Life continues.

OUTCOMES

I am not responsible for your outcomes.

I do not charm them
        Nor cajole them.
I do not entreaty them
        Nor coerce them.
I do not intimidate,
        Subjugate, interrogate
        Instigate.

Your outcomes are yours alone,
Born of your perceptions,
Your dreams, your fears,
Your experiences, your history,
Your path.

Sometimes we coincide (nice!).
But we never commingle,
For you are on your path
And I am on mine.

I cannot fail you
Nor you me.
Failure and achievement
We do for ourselves.

No Fear

We were together in a way
That brought me joy.

Perhaps we will not be together
That way again.

But I do not owe you my Fear.

A BUMPY RIDE

Romantic love creates disequilibrium.
We soar. We plummet.

Why?
Because we are attached
To someone else's wings.

We fly.
But only if we ride the same current.

DAVIDA, MY SOUL

Davida, My Soul, is of God.
She is not God.
She is *of* God.

She knows what I need.
She does not force,
But she is always accessible.

I learn to take time to hear Davida.

I learn to take time to her
For she is timeless.

WHAT COULD BE SOFTER?

Take your heart forward
Into Rosewood
And Sandalwood
And would-would.

Or could.

But let go of should.

BLINK

I think a flower
Is the most beautiful thing I've ever seen.
(My eyes are so tiny!)

Senseless

Why do I have so much trouble meeting God
When He is everywhere?

Drat these senses that
Try to stuff God into a five-sided box!
He is so much more.

Only the Dweller Within,
My Soul, My Davida,
Can perceive Him.

The One and the Many

I can see one suffer
And know.
I can see many suffer
And not know.

The magnitude overwhelms,
But the single example teaches.
One man commits sin
And sin becomes possible
(Replication adds no significance).

So as you do unto the least of them,
So you do unto me.

Before I knew of animals' misery,
Did I have peace?
I think I had only ignorance.
Now, simply having thought of their condition,
I'm changed.

ONE HAND CLAPPING

The woodpecker embodies all things,
In my mind, everything is the woodpecker .

When he rattles, I affirm him.
When he does not rattle, I make him up
(Even though I do not see him).

My thought is the woodpecker.

Before I ever saw him,
I knew him.
Then I made him more and more.

Now I make him come and go.
Just when I think of him,
He rattles.

How do I make all things happen?
(How do I think of the woodpecker?)

Perhaps...

We all choose when to die.

A Little Guidance

Always, and for all time, do these three:

1. Tell the truth and tell it with loving intent, for The Truth shall set you free.

2. Remember Who You Really Are—one perfect dimension of the hologram of God.

3. Choose over and over again to do that—and only that—which reflects Who You Really Are.

IT MATTERS, BECAUSE ...

What we tolerate.
We encourage.